solar system

JUPITER

AND

SATURN

Rosalind Mist

QEB Publishing

Words in **bold** can be found in the glossary on page 22.

Library of Congress Control Number:
2008012589

ISBN 978-1-59566-581-2

Printed and bound in the United States

Author Rosalind Mist
Consultant Terry Jennings
Editor Amanda Askew
Designer Melissa Alaverdy
Picture Researcher Maria Joannou

Publisher Steve Evans
Creative Director Zeta Davies

Picture credits
(fc=front cover, t=top, b=bottom, l=left, r=right)

Corbis NASA/Roger Ressmeyer 8r, Xinhua 5t

ESA 12l, 18l, 19, 20t, 21b, NASA 18r

NASA fc, The Hubble Heritage Team (STScI/
AURA) 1b, JPL/Space Science Institute 1t, 10,
11t, 15b, 16–17, 20b, 21t, 24, Johns Hopkins U
APL/SWRI 11b, Hubble Heritage Team (STScI/
AURA) 15t, JPL 2, 8l, 14, 23, JPL/DLR 9, JPL/Space
Science Institute 12r, JPL/University of Arizona
13t, JPL/University of Arizona 13t, NSSDC 6–7,
Reta Beebe (New Mexico State University)/
D Gilmore, L Bergeron (STScI) 13b

Shutterstock 2–3, 4b, 4–5

Contents

The Solar System

The **Solar System is made up of the Sun, and everything that** orbits, **or circles, it.**
This includes the planets and their moons, as well as **meteors, asteroids,** and **comets.**

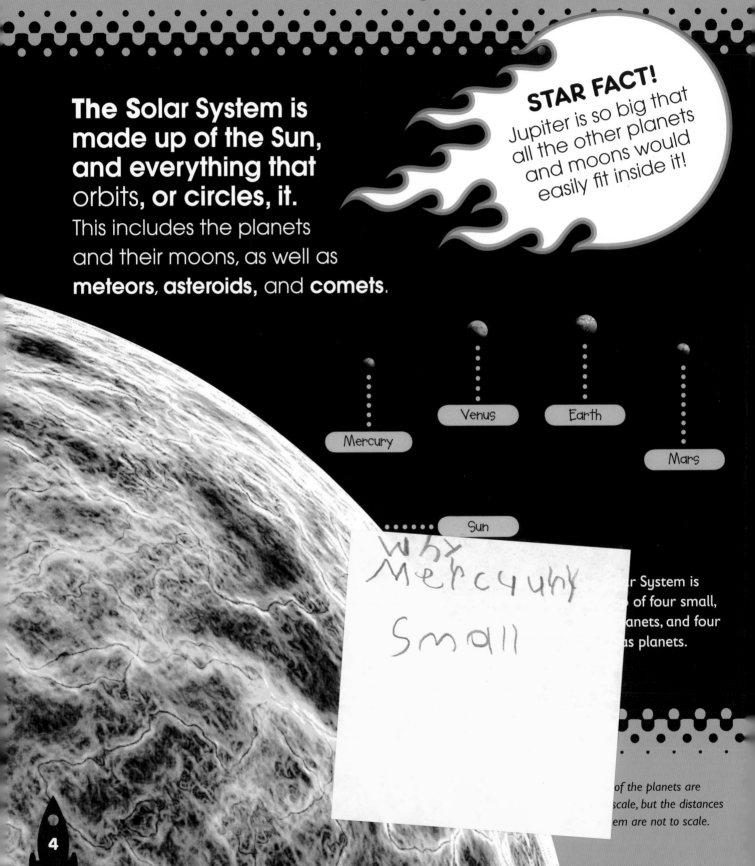

STAR FACT!
Jupiter is so big that all the other planets and moons would easily fit inside it!

Mercury

Venus

Earth

Mars

Sun

why Mercury small

...r System is ... of four small, ...anets, and four ...as planets.

...of the planets are ...scale, but the distances ...em are not to scale.

4

The Solar System is held together by an invisible force called **gravity**. On Earth, gravity stops people from floating into space!

 Astronauts find out what it feels like to be weightless in space in a special plane. It is nicknamed the "vomit comet" because people often feel ill on the flight.

Saturn

Neptune

Uranus

Jupiter

The Sun and planets in the Solar System were formed billions of years ago. They were made of gas and dust. The Sun is star that formed about five billion years ago. There are eight planets Mars, Jupiter,

why do Peeqple fly

Jupiter

Jupiter is the largest planet in the Solar System.
It is actually bigger than all the other planets put together. Although you could fit 1,321 Earths inside it, Jupiter is still smaller than the Sun. The only solid part of Jupiter is its small, rocky core, or middle. The rest of it is made of gas. All that can be seen are clouds.

Jupiter

Earth

Jupiter is the fifth planet from the Sun, between Mars and Saturn. It is a long way from the Sun—five times further from the Sun than Earth.

For such a large planet, Jupiter spins around quickly. A day on Jupiter only lasts for about ten hours!

STAR FACT!
The ancient Greeks named the planet Zeus after the king of their gods. "Jupiter" is the Roman name for Zeus.

How big is Jupiter?

· · · · · · · · · · · · · · ·

Make your own fruit-and-vegetable
Solar System to show the different sizes
(not the shapes) of the planets.

Small bean (Mercury)   Grapefruit (Jupiter)
Grape (Venus)   Orange (Saturn)
Cherry (Earth)   Peach (Uranus)
Pea (Mars)   Plum (Neptune)

Using this scale, the Sun is more than
3 feet across—bigger than
a hula hoop!

 Jupiter is about 11 times wider
than the Earth, but the Sun is
ten times wider than Jupiter!

Jupiter's moons

Jupiter has more than 63 moons.
They are all different sizes and 14 of them were discovered so recently that they do not yet have names. Four of Jupiter's moons are so big that they can be seen from Earth with a small **telescope**.

whxis theher poksin saapqs

... moon to ... rful with lots ... Some of the ... than Earth's ... ount Everest. ... ce a ... **r**, ... **or**.

The volcanoes on Io are hotter than anything else in the Solar System, apart from the Sun.

Io does not have many **craters** because the surface is slowly being covered by **lava**.

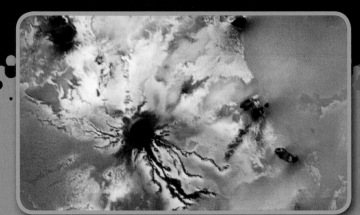

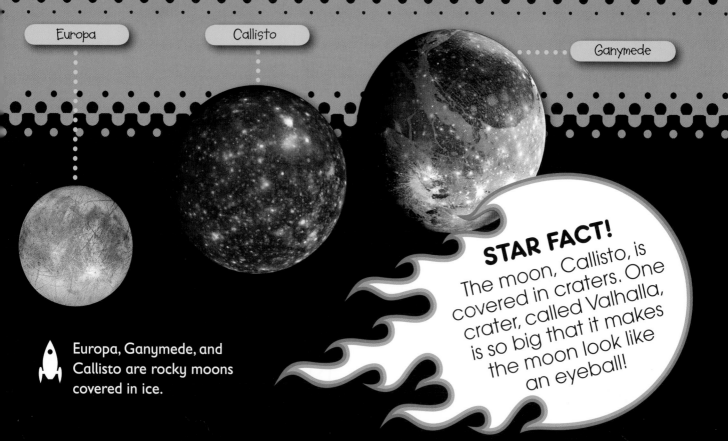

Europa

Callisto

Ganymede

Europa, Ganymede, and Callisto are rocky moons covered in ice.

STAR FACT!
The moon, Callisto, is covered in craters. One crater, called Valhalla, is so big that it makes the moon look like an eyeball!

Ganymede is the largest Moon in the Solar System. Europa is the smallest of the four main moons. Callisto is in between, about the same size as Mercury. Scientists think that there might be oceans underneath the ice on these moons. A future mission to Jupiter may send a robot to explore Europa.

Galileo Galilei

In 1610, Italian **astronomer** Galileo Galilei discovered Jupiter's four biggest moons—Io, Europa, Ganymede, and Callisto. This is why they are called the Galilean Moons. From 1995 to 2003, the *Galileo* **space probe** orbited, or circled, Jupiter and sent back information about the planet and its moons.

Cloudy planets

Jupiter and Saturn look like giant clouds.

Space probes cannot land on the gas planets because there is nothing to land on.

 On Jupiter, the bright clouds are higher in the **atmosphere** and colder. They are made of crystals of **ammonia**. The dark clouds are lower down in the atmosphere.

Jupiter and Saturn spin very quickly. They both take about ten hours to spin around once. This fast spinning makes their clouds line up in colored bands and so the planets look striped. It also makes them bulge around the middle.

STAR FACT!
Jupiter seems to be made of similar things to the Sun. It is a bit like a star that never became big enough to start burning.

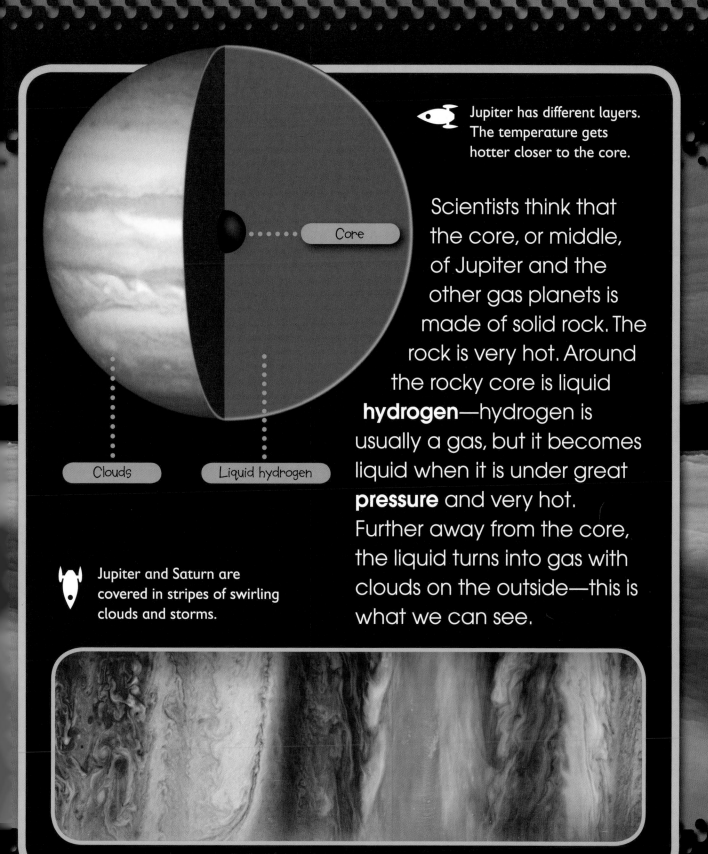

Core

Clouds

Liquid hydrogen

Jupiter has different layers. The temperature gets hotter closer to the core.

Scientists think that the core, or middle, of Jupiter and the other gas planets is made of solid rock. The rock is very hot. Around the rocky core is liquid **hydrogen**—hydrogen is usually a gas, but it becomes liquid when it is under great **pressure** and very hot. Further away from the core, the liquid turns into gas with clouds on the outside—this is what we can see.

Jupiter and Saturn are covered in stripes of swirling clouds and storms.

Stormy weather

One of the most incredible things about Jupiter is that it has a large storm called the Great Red Spot.

This giant swirl of red clouds is more than 24,800 miles across—three times the size of Earth. Scientists have been able to see the Great Red Spot for more than 300 years.

Great Red Spot

Jupiter and Saturn both have **lightning** storms. These are much bigger than lightning storms on Earth.

STAR FACT!

Temperatures at the top of Jupiter's clouds can drop to -240 degrees Fahrenheit. That's much colder than the coldest place on Earth.

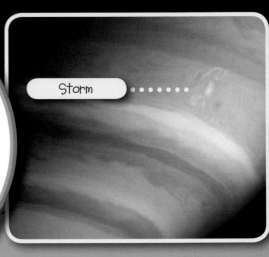

Storm

 The Dragon Storm on Saturn has bright clouds and lightning.

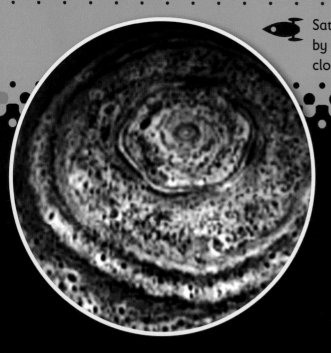

Saturn's north pole is surrounded by clouds with six sides! These clouds are 45 miles deep.

Winds on Saturn are six times stronger than the strongest hurricanes on Earth—they can travel at 1,100 miles an hour!

Saturn has storms, too, but none as big as the Great Red Spot. The strangest storm found on Saturn has six sides, like honeycomb!

Storm

Round and round

· · · · · · · · · · · · ·

Fill a clear tumbler halfway with water. Stir in different glitters. Swirl the water in the tumbler. You will see the glitter line up in circles on the surface and in the water. Jupiter and Saturn's clouds line up like this.

This is a white, arrowhead-shaped storm on Saturn. The storm is about the size of Earth.

Saturn

Saturn is the sixth planet from the Sun and is also a gas planet with a small, rocky core, or middle.

Saturn is ten times further from the Sun than Earth. Although Saturn is smaller than Jupiter, it is still massive. It is so big that 763 Earths could fit inside it.

Saturn

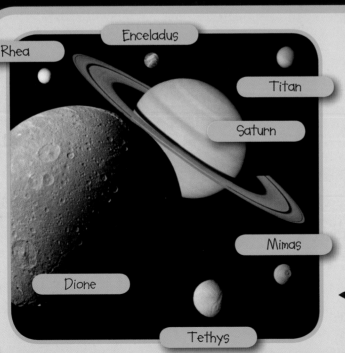

Rhea

Enceladus

Titan

Saturn

Dione

Mimas

Tethys

Saturn has more than 60 moons. Saturn also has rings. They circle around the middle of the planet and were discovered by an astronomer called Christiaan Huygens more than 300 years ago.

 The *Voyager 1* space probe flew by Saturn in 1980 and took pictures of the planet's six main moons.

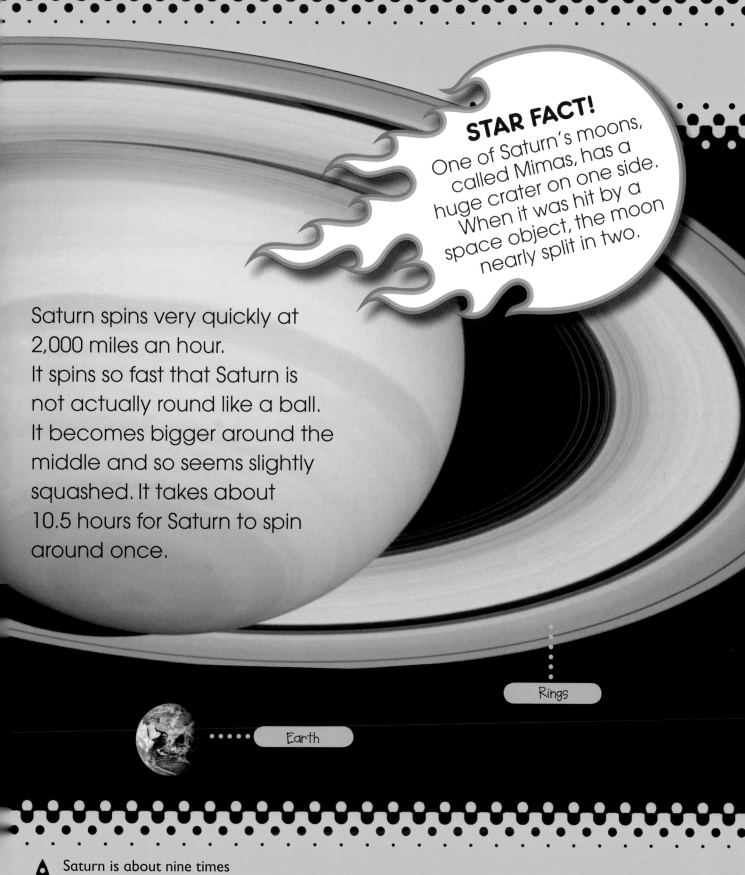

Saturn spins very quickly at 2,000 miles an hour.
It spins so fast that Saturn is not actually round like a ball.
It becomes bigger around the middle and so seems slightly squashed. It takes about 10.5 hours for Saturn to spin around once.

Rings

Earth

Saturn is about nine times larger than the Earth and with its rings it is 21 times wider.

Saturn's rings

Saturn is not the only planet to have rings—all the gas planets have rings. The rings are made from millions of pieces of rock and ice that move around the planet. The pieces are all different sizes—from the size of a grain of sand to the size of a car! The rock and ice in the rings probably came from comets, asteroids, or moons that got too close to the planet and broke up.

As Saturn orbits the Sun, the top, the edge, and then the bottom of the rings can be seen from Earth. This makes the rings look like they are changing shape.

Some of the rings are bright and seem to be full of tiny bits of dust, rock, and ice. Others are dull in color and seem emptier.

The rings are very wide, but thin. They stretch 168,000 miles across, but are only about 65 feet in thickness. If the rings were only as thick as a sheet of paper, they would still be 4,200 feet across!

Saturn's rings

Cut a donut shape out of card and decorate it with glitter.
Stick cocktail sticks around the middle of a grapefruit, then stick the card to the cocktail sticks.
Tilt your model to see how the shimmering rings seem to change shape!

Cassini-Huygens

Saturn

Cassini

Cassini-Huygens is a space probe that explored Saturn, its rings, and moons.
A probe is a **spacecraft** that does not carry people. It is sent into space to collect information about a planet or moon.

Cassini-Huygens was launched in 1997. The space probe traveled 2.2 billion miles to reach Saturn. This is more than 9,000 times further than the Moon is from Earth. It took seven years for the probe to get there.

 By the end of 2008, *Cassini* had orbited Saturn 74 times and flown past some of its moons, including Titan.

 Cassini-Huygens was launched into space using a rocket.

Cassini and Huygens

The *Cassini-Huygens* probe is named after two famous astronomers. In 1655, Christiaan Huygens discovered Titan, the first moon around Saturn. In 1675, Giovanni Cassini discovered a gap between Saturn's rings.

STAR FACT!

When *Cassini* arrived at Saturn, it had to fly through a gap in the rings so it could orbit the planet.

The cameras and other science equipment on board *Cassini* helped scientists to find out more about Saturn. Scientists have discovered about 30 new moons and more rings around Saturn. They have even seen fierce lightning storms.

Cassini-Huygens was enormous, about the size of a bus. It was actually two space probes in one. *Cassini* orbited Saturn, and *Huygens* landed on Saturn's largest moon, Titan.

 Huygens was released from *Cassini* by a spring. After 20 days, it went through Titan's atmosphere and floated to the surface using a parachute.

Titan

Saturn's largest moon is called Titan.
It is the only moon in the Solar System with a thick atmosphere and clouds.

The *Cassini-Huygens* space probe arrived at Saturn in 2004. *Huygens* landed on Titan on January 14, 2005. Parachutes were used to slow down the probe before it landed on Titan.

 Once *Huygens* had slowed down enough, it started to send information to *Cassini*.

 Titan is like Venus. Its clouds are so thick that you cannot see through them.

The probe discovered large lakes, rivers, seas, and land. Titan is very cold, so any water freezes. The seas are actually made up of liquid **methane** —methane is normally a gas, but it turns into a liquid when it is very cold.

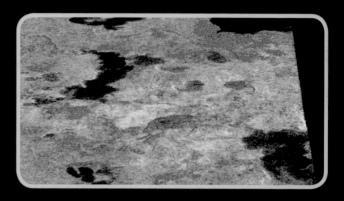

 Cassini found lakes of liquid methane on the surface of Titan.

The space probe also discovered giant dunes, which are like hills, made of tiny pieces of ice and other materials.

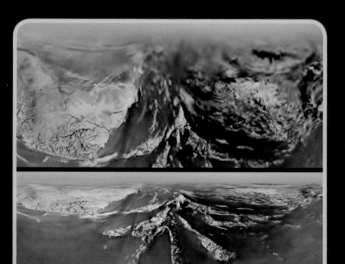

STAR FACT!
Huygens used a parachute that measured 26 feet across to float down to Titan. It took more than two hours!

 Huygens took pictures of Titan's surface. These pictures show mountains, valleys, riverbeds, and clouds.

Glossary

Active volcano
A volcano—a place where liquid rock called magma comes to the surface —that can still erupt.

Ammonia
A smelly gas.

Asteroid
A large lump of rock, too small to be a planet or dwarf planet.

Astronaut
A person who travels in space.

Astronomer
A scientist who studies the Solar System, stars, and galaxies.

Atmosphere
A layer of gases around a planet or moon.

Comet
An object in space made of rock and ice.

Crater
A hole made on the surface of a planet or moon by an asteroid or comet.

Gas
A substance, such as air, that is not solid or liquid. Gas cannot usually be seen.

Gravity
Attractive pulling force between any massive objects.

Hydrogen
The lightest gas.

Lava
Molten, or liquid, rock that has cooled and turned into a solid.

Lightning
An enormous spark of electricity traveling through the atmosphere.

Meteor
A glowing trail in the sky left by a small piece of rock from space.

Methane
Natural gas.

Orbit
The path of one body around another, such as a planet around the Sun.

Pressure
When something is pressed or squeezed.

Spacecraft
A vehicle that travels in space.

Space probe
A spacecraft without people on board.

Sulfur
A solid, yellow chemical.

Telescope
An instrument you look through that makes things in the distance seem large.

Index

Notes for parents and teachers

- Jupiter and Saturn have large magnetic fields, which stretch out into space a long way.

- Saturn and Jupiter's clouds spin around the planet at different speeds, depending on how far they are from the Equator.

- Scientists use a parachute to slow down spacecraft where there is an atmosphere, such as on Titan. This does not work on planets, moons, or asteroids without a thick atmosphere. In these cases, scientists have to use rockets to change the speed of the spacecraft.

- The rings of Saturn are one of the most beautiful sights in the Universe. You can find out where Saturn is in the sky by looking on the Internet at www.skyandtelescope.com/observing/ataglance* or in a newspaper. It is sometimes possible to see the rings through a very good pair of stabilized binoculars, but to see them clearly, you will need to use a good telescope.

- Without a parachute, space probes would fall faster and faster towards the planet or moon that they were visiting. Parachutes cover a large area. The air resistance against the parachute balances against the force of gravity of the falling object, and stops it falling faster.

- To illustrate how air resistance is related to area, try dropping a flat piece of paper, and see how long it takes to fall to the ground. Now scrunch it up and drop it. It falls to the ground much faster, as it has a smaller area being affected by air resistance.

*Website information is correct at time of going to press. However, the publishers cannot accept liability for any information or links found on third-party websites.